God makes the rivers to flow.
They tire not, nor do they cease from flowing.
May the river of my life
flow into the sea of love that is the Lord.

Nilgiri Press

# God Makes the Rivers to Flow • *Passages for Meditation*

## Selected by Eknath Easwaran

*Other books by Eknath Easwaran*

Gandhi the Man

The Bhagavad Gita for Daily Living

    1. The End of Sorrow

    2. Like a Thousand Suns

The Mantram Handbook

Meditation

Dialogue with Death

The Supreme Ambition

© *1982 by the Blue Mountain Center of Meditation*
*All rights reserved. Manufactured in the United States of America*
*Designed, printed, and bound at Nilgiri Press*
*First printing August, 1982*
*ISBN: case 0–915132–28–1, paper 0–915132–29–X*

*The Blue Mountain Center of Meditation, founded in Berkeley*
*in 1960 by Eknath Easwaran, publishes books on how to lead the*
*spiritual life in the home and the community. For information*
*please write to Nilgiri Press, Box 477, Petaluma, California 94953.*

*Library of Congress Cataloging in Publication Data:*

*Easwaran, Eknath.*
    *God makes the rivers to flow.*

    *Includes bibliographical references.*
    *1. Meditations.    I. Title.*
*BL624.E16   1982    291.4′3    82–8101*
*ISBN 0–915132–28–1       AACR2*
*ISBN 0–915132–29–X (pbk.)*

# Acknowledgments

We are grateful to the following publishers for permission to reprint selections from their books:

Navajivan Trust for "The Path" (p. 59), from M. K. Gandhi, *My Religion* (Ahmedabad: Navajivan, 1955)

Ramakrishna-Vivekananda Center for "Songs from Ramakrishna" (pp. 80–81), from *The Gospel of Sri Ramakrishna,* by "M.", translated by Swami Nikhilananda (copyright 1942 by Swami Nikhilananda: Ramakrishna-Vivekananda Center of New York, 1942); and for the "last message" of Sri Sarada Devi (p. 59), "The Whole World Is Your Own," from *Holy Mother* by Swami Nikhilananda (copyright 1962 by Swami Nikhilananda: Ramakrishna-Vivekananda Center of New York, 1962)

The Vedanta Society of Southern California for "Invocations to the Upanishads," from *The Upanishads: Breath of the Eternal,* translated by Swami Prabhavananda and Frederick Manchester (Hollywood: Vedanta Press, 1968); and for "May We Be United in Heart" (p. 29) and "Hymn to the Divine Mother" (p. 31), from *Prayers and Meditations Compiled from the Scriptures of India,* edited by Swami Prabhavananda and Clive Johnson (Hollywood: Vedanta Press, 1967)

Other sources and translators are mentioned in the Notes.

# Table of Contents

Eknath Easwaran
## *Introduction*

*(T) 9-28-82*

In ancient India lived a sculptor renowned for his life-sized statues of elephants. With trunks curled high, tusks thrust forward, thick legs trampling the earth, these carved beasts seemed to trumpet to the sky. One day, a king came to see these magnificent works and to commission statuary for his palace. Struck with wonder, he asked the sculptor, "What is the secret of your artistry?"

The sculptor quietly took his measure of the monarch and replied, "Great king, when with the aid of many men I quarry a gigantic piece of granite from the banks of the river, I have it set here in my courtyard. For a long time, I do nothing but observe this block of stone and study it from every angle. I focus all my concentration on this task and won't allow anything or anybody to disturb me. At first, I see nothing but a huge and shapeless rock sitting there, meaningless, indifferent to my purposes, utterly out of place. It seems faintly resentful at having been dragged from its cool place by the rushing waters. Then, slowly, very slowly, I begin to notice something in the substance of the rock. I feel a presentiment . . . an outline, scarcely discernible, shows itself to me, though others, I suspect, would perceive nothing. I watch with an open eye and a joyous, eager heart. The outline grows stronger. Oh, yes, I can see it! An elephant is stirring in there!

"Only then do I start to work. For days flowing into weeks I use my chisel and mallet, always clinging to my sense of that outline, which grows ever stronger. How the big fellow strains! How he yearns to be out! How he wants to live! It seems so clear now, for I know the one thing I must do: with an utter singleness of purpose, I must chip away every last bit of stone that is *not* elephant. What then remains will be, must be, elephant."

When I was young, my Grandmother, my spiritual guide, would often tell just such a story, not only to entertain but to convey the essential truths of living. Perhaps I had asked her, as revered teachers in every religion have been asked, "What happens in the spiritual life? What are we supposed to do?"

My Granny wasn't a theologian, so she answered these questions simply with a story like that of the elephant sculptor. She was showing that we do not need to bring our real self, our higher self, into existence. It is already there. It has always been there, yearning to be out. An incomparable spark of divinity is to be found in the heart of each human being, waiting to radiate love and wisdom everywhere, because that is its nature. Amazing! This you that sometimes feels inadequate, sometimes becomes afraid or angry or depressed, that searches on and on for fulfillment, contains within itself the very fulfillment it seeks, and to a supreme degree.

Indeed, the tranquility and happiness we also feel are actually reflections of that inner reality of which we know so little. No matter what mistakes we may have made—and who hasn't made them?—this true self is ever pure and unsullied. No matter what trouble we have caused ourselves and those around us, this true self is ceaselessly loving. No matter how time passes from us and with it the body in which we dwell, this true self is beyond change, eternal.

Once we have become attentive to the presence of this true self, then all we really need do is resolutely chip away whatever is not divine in ourselves. I am not saying this is easy or quick. Quite the contrary; it can't be done in a week or by the weak. But the task is clearly laid out before us. By removing that which is petty and self-seeking, we bring forth all that is glorious and mindful of the whole. In this there is no loss, only gain. The chips pried away are of no consequence when compared to the magnificence of what will emerge. Can you imagine a sculptor scurrying to pick up the slivers that fall from his chisel, hoarding them, treasuring them, ignoring the statue altogether? Just so, when we get even a glimpse of the splendor of our inner being, our beloved preoccupations, predilections, and peccadillos will lose their glamour and seem utterly drab.

What remains when all that is not divine drops away is summed up in the short Sanskrit word *aroga*. The prefix *a* signifies "not a trace of"; *roga* means "illness" or "incapacity." Actually, the word loses some of its thrust in translation. In the original it connotes perfect well-being, not mere freedom from sickness. Often, you know, we say, "I'm well," when all we mean is that we haven't taken to our bed with a bottle of cough syrup, a vaporizer, and a pitcher of fruit juice—we're getting about, more or less. But perhaps we have been so far from optimum functioning for so long that we don't realize what splendid health we are capable of. This *aroga* of the spiritual life entails the complete removal of every obstacle to impeccable health, giving us a strong and energetic body, a clear mind, positive emotions, and a heart radiant with love. When we have such soundness, we are always secure, always considerate, good to be around. Our relationships flourish, and we become a boon to the earth, not a burden on it.

Every time I reflect on this, I am filled with wonder. Voices can be heard crying out that human nature is debased, that everything is meaningless, that there is nothing we can do, but the mystics of every religion testify otherwise. They assure us that in every country, under adverse circumstances and favorable, ordinary people like you and me have taken on the immense challenge of the spiritual life and made this supreme discovery. They have found out who awaits them within the body, within the mind, within the spirit of man.

Consider the case of Francis Bernardone, who lived in Italy in the thirteenth century. I'm focusing on him because we know that at the beginning he was quite an ordinary young man. By day this son of a rich cloth merchant, a bit of a popinjay, lived the life of the privileged, with its games, its position, its pleasures. By night, feeling all the vigor of youth, he strolled the streets of Assisi with his lute, crooning love ballads beneath candle-lit balconies. Life was sweet, if shallow. But then the same force, the same dazzling inner light, that cast Saul of Tarsus to the earth and made him cry out, "Not I! Not I! But Christ liveth in me!"—just such a force plunges our troubadour deep within, wrenching loose all his old ways. He hears the irresistible voice of his God calling to him through a crucifix, "Francis, Francis, rebuild my church." And this meant not only the Chapel of San Damiano that lay in ruins nearby, not only the whole of the Church, but that which was closest of all—the man himself.

This tremendous turnabout in consciousness is compressed into the Prayer of Saint Francis. Whenever we repeat it, we are immersing ourselves in the spiritual wisdom of a holy lifetime. Here is the opening:

> Lord, make me an instrument of thy peace.
> Where there is hatred, let me sow love.

These lines are so deep that no one will ever fathom them. Profound, bottomless, they express the infinity of the Self. As you grow spiritually, they will mean more and more to you, without end.

But a very practical question arises here. Even if we recognize their great depth, we all know how terribly difficult it is to practice them in the constant give and take of life. For more than twenty years, I have heard people, young and old, say that they respond to such magnificent words—that is just how they would like to be—but they don't know how to do it; it seems so far beyond their reach. In the presence of such spiritual wisdom, we feel so frail, so driven by personal concerns, that we think we can never, never become like Saint Francis of Assisi.

I say to them, "There is a way." I tell them that we *can* change all that is selfish in us into selfless, all that is impure in us into pure, all that is unsightly into beauty. Happily, whatever our tradition, we are inheritors of straightforward spiritual practices whose power can be proved by anyone. These practices vary a bit from culture to culture, as you would expect, but essentially they are the same. Such practices are our sculptor's tools for carving away what is not-us so the real us can emerge.

Meditation is supreme among all these tested means for personal change. Nothing is so direct, so potent, so sure for releasing the divinity within us. Meditation enables us to see the lineaments of our true self and to chip away the stubbornly selfish tendencies that keep it locked within, quite, quite forgotten.

In meditation, the inspirational passage is the chisel, our concentration is the hammer, and our resolute will delivers the blows. And how the pieces fly! A very small, fine chisel edge, as you know, can wedge away huge chunks of stone. As with the other basic tools of man—the lever, the pulley—we gain tremendous advantages of force. When we use our will to drive the thin edge of the passage deep into consciousness, we get the purchase to pry loose tenacious habits and negative attitudes. The passage, whether it is from the Bhagavad Gita or *The Imitation of Christ* or the Dhammapada of the Buddha, has been tempered in the flames of mystical experience, and its bite will . . . well, try it and find out for yourself just what it can do. In the end, only such personal experience persuades.

Now if we could hold an interview with a negative tendency, say, Resentment, it might say, "I don't worry! I've been safely settled in this fellow's mind for years. He takes good care of me—feeds me, dwells on me, brings me out and parades me around! All I have to do is roar and stir things up from time to time. Yes, I'm getting huge and feeling grand. And I'm proud to tell you there are even a few little rancors and vituperations running around now, spawned by yours truly!" So he may think. But I assure you that when you meditate on the glorious words of Saint Francis, you are prying him loose. You are saying in a way that goes beyond vows and good intentions that resentment is no part of you. You no longer acknowledge its right to exist. Thus, we bring ever more perceptibly into view our divine self. We use something genuine to drive out impostors that have roamed about largely through our neglect and helplessness.

To meditate and live the spiritual life, we needn't drop everything and undertake an ascent of the Himalayas or Mount Athos or Cold Mountain. There are some who like to imagine themselves as pilgrims moving among the deer on high forest paths, simply-clad, sipping only pure headwaters, breathing only ethereal mountain air. Now it may sound unglamorous, but you can actually do better right where you are. Your situation may lack the grandeur of those austere and solitary peaks, but it could be a very fertile valley yielding marvelous fruit. We need people if we are to grow, and all our problems with them, properly seen, are opportunities for growth. Can you practice patience with a deer? Can you learn to forgive a redwood? But trying to live in harmony with those around you right now will bring out enormous inner toughness. Your powerful elephant will stir and come to life.

The old dispute about the relative virtues of the active way and the contemplative way is a spurious one. We require both. They are phases of a single rhythm like the pulsing of the heart, the in-drawing and letting go of breath, the ebb and flow of the tides. So we go deep, deep inwards in meditation to consolidate our vital energy, and then with greater love and wisdom we come out into the family, the community, the world. Without action we lack opportunities for changing our old ways, and we increase our self-will rather than lessen it; without contemplation we lack the strength to change and are blown about by our conditioning. When we meditate every day and also do our best in every situation, we walk both worthy roads, the *via contemplativa* and the *via activa*.

The passages in this book are *meant* for meditation. So used, they can lead us deep into our minds where the transformation of all that is selfish in us must take place. Simply reading them may console us, it may inspire us, but it cannot bring about fundamental, lasting change; meditation alone does that. Only meditation, so far as I know, can release the inner resources locked within us, and put before us problems worthy of those resources. Only meditation gives such a vital edge to life. This is maturity. This is coming into our own, as our concerns deepen and broaden, dwarfing the personal satisfactions—and worries—that once meant so much to us.

If you want to know how to use inspirational passages in meditation, I refer you to my other books, especially *Meditation,* where detailed instructions are given. The basic technique, duration and pace, posture, place, and problems are all taken up. You will also find there a complete eight-point program for spiritual living, including the use of the mantram, slowing down, and achieving one-pointed attention. I would like here, though, to say a bit about the criteria I have used in selecting these particular passages.

We wouldn't use a dull chisel or one meant for wood on a piece of stone, and we should use suitable passages for meditation. We're not after intellectual knowledge, which helps us understand and manipulate the external world. We seek spiritual wisdom, which leads to inner awareness. There the separate strands of the external world—the people, the beasts and birds and fish, the trees and grasses, the moving waters and still, the earth itself—are brought into one great interconnected cord of life, and we find the will to live in accordance with that awareness. We find the will to live in perpetual love. I think you'll agree there are very few books which can ever lead us to that.

The test of suitable meditation passages is simply this: Does the passage bear the imprint of deep, personal spiritual experience? Is it the statement of one who went beyond the narrow confines of past conditioning into the unfathomable recesses of the mind, there to begin the great work of transformation? This is the unmistakable stamp of authenticity. Only such precious writings can speak directly to our heart and soul. Their very words are invested with validity; we feel we are in the presence of the genuine.

The scriptures of the world's religions certainly meet this test, and so do the statements of passionate lovers of God like Saint Teresa, Kabir, Sri Ramakrishna, Ansari of Herat. And whatever lacks this validation by personal experience, however poetic or imaginative, however speculative or novel, is not suited for use in meditation.

But there is another thing to be considered: is the passage positive, inspirational, life-affirming? We should avoid passages from whatever source that are negative, that stress our foolish errors rather than our enduring strength and wisdom, or that deprecate life in the world, which is precisely where we must do our living. Instead let us choose passages that hold steadily before us a radiant image of the true Self we are striving to realize.

For the great principle upon which meditation rests is that we become what we meditate on. Actually, even in everyday life we are shaped by what gains our attention and occupies our thoughts. If we spend time studying the market, checking the money rates, evaluating our portfolios, we are going to become money-people. Anyone looking sensitively into our eyes will see two big dollar signs, and we'll look out at the world through them, too. Attention can be caught in so many things: food, books, collections, travel, television. The Buddha put it succinctly: "All that we are is the result of what we have thought."

If this is true of daily life, it is even more so in meditation, which is concentration itself. In the hours spent in meditation we are removing many years of the "what we have thought." At that time we need the most powerful tools we can find for accomplishing the task. That is why in selecting passages, I have aimed for the highest the human being is capable of, the most noble and elevating truths that have ever been expressed on this planet. Our petty selfishness, our vain illusions, simply must and will give way under the power of these universal principles of life, as sand castles erode before the surge of the sea.

Specifically, what happens in meditation is that we slow down the furious, fragmented activity of the mind and lead it to a measured, sustained focus on what we want to become. Under the impact of a rapidly-moving, conditioned mind, we lose our sense of freely choosing. But as the mind slows down, we begin to gain control of it in daily life. Many habitual responses in what we eat, see, and do, and in the ways we relate to people, come under our inspection and governance. We realize that we have choices. This is profoundly liberating and takes away every trace of boredom and depression.

The passages in this collection have been drawn from many traditions, and you'll find considerable variety among them. Some are in verse, some in prose; some are from the East, some from the West; some are ancient, some quite recent; some stress love, some insight, some good works. So there are differences, yes, in tone, theme, cultural milieu, but they all have this in common: they will work.

As your meditation progresses, I encourage you to build a varied repertory of passages to guard against overfamiliarity, where the repetition can become somewhat mechanical. In this way, you can match a passage to your particular need at the time—the inspiration, the reminder, the reassurance most meaningful to you.

Nearly everyone has had some longing to be an artist and can feel some affinity with my Granny's elephant sculptor. Most of us probably spent some time at painting, writing, dancing, or music-making. Whether it has fallen away, or we still keep our hand in, we remember our touches with the great world of art, a world of beauty and harmony, of similitudes and stark contrasts, of repetition and variation, of compelling rhythms like those of the cosmos itself. We know, too, that while we can all appreciate art, only a few can create masterworks or perform them as virtuosi.

Now I wish to invite you to undertake the greatest art
work of all, an undertaking which *is* for everyone, forever,
never to be put aside, even for a single day. I speak of the
purpose of our life, the thing without which every other goal
or achievement will lose its meaning and turn to ashes. I invite you to step back and look with your artist's eye at your
own life. Consider it amorphous material, not yet deliberately
crafted. Reflect upon what it is, and what it could be. Imagine
how you will feel, and what those around you will lose, if it
does not become what it could be. Observe that you have
been given two marvelous instruments of love and service:
the external instrument, this intricate network of systems that
is the body; the internal, this subtle and versatile mind. Pon-
der the deeds they have given rise to, and the deeds they
can give rise to.

And set to work. Sit for meditation, and sit again. Every
day without fail, sick or well, tired or energetic, alone or with
others, at home or away from home, sit for meditation, as
great artists throw themselves into their creations. As you sit,
you will have in hand the supreme hammer and chisel; use
it to hew away all unwanted effects of your heredity, conditioning, environment, and latencies. Bring forth the noble
work of art within you! My earnest wish is that one day
you shall see in all its purity the effulgent spiritual being
you really are.

*May the thread of my song be not cut*
*before my life merges in the sea of love*

*Part One*

# *The Prayer of Saint Francis*

Lord, make me an instrument of thy peace.
Where there is hatred, let me sow love;
Where there is injury, pardon;
Where there is doubt, faith;
Where there is despair, hope;
Where there is darkness, light;
Where there is sadness, joy.

O divine Master, grant that I may not so much seek
To be consoled as to console,
To be understood as to understand,
To be loved as to love;
For it is in giving that we receive;
It is in pardoning that we are pardoned;
It is in dying [to self] that we are born to eternal life.

# Invocations to the Upanishads

*Lead me from the unreal to the real.*
*Lead me from darkness to light.*
*Lead me from death to immortality.*

## 1

May the Lord of Love protect us.
May the Lord of Love nourish us.
May the Lord of Love strengthen us.
May we realize the Lord of Love.
May we live with love for all;
May we live in peace with all.
OM   *Shānti Shānti Shānti*

## 2

May the Lord of day grant us peace.
May the Lord of night grant us peace.
May the Lord of sight grant us peace.
May the Lord of might grant us peace.
May the Lord of speech grant us peace.
May the Lord of space grant us peace.
I bow down to Brahman, source of all power.
I will speak the truth and follow the law.
Guard me and my teacher against all harm.
Guard me and my teacher against all harm.
OM   *Shānti Shānti Shānti*

**3**

Filled with Brahman are the things we see,
Filled with Brahman are the things we see not,
From out of Brahman floweth all that is:
From Brahman all — yet is he still the same.
OM  *Shānti Shānti Shānti*

**4**

May quietness descend upon my limbs,
My speech, my breath, my eyes, my ears;
May all my senses wax clear and strong.
May Brahman show himself unto me.
Never may I deny Brahman, nor Brahman me.
I with him and he with me —
    may we abide always together.
May there be revealed to me,
Who am devoted to Brahman,
The holy truth of the Upanishads.
OM  *Shānti Shānti Shānti*

**5**

OM
With our ears may we hear what is good.
With our eyes may we behold thy righteousness.
Tranquil in body, may we who worship thee find rest.
OM  *Shānti Shānti Shānti*
OM. . . Hail to the supreme Self!

**6**

May my speech be one with my mind,
    and may my mind be one with my speech.
O thou self-luminous Brahman,
    remove the veil of ignorance from before me,
    that I may behold thy light.
Do thou reveal to me
    the spirit of the scriptures.
May the truth of the scriptures
    be ever present to me.
May I seek day and night to realize
    what I learn from the sages.
May I speak the truth of Brahman.
May I speak the truth.
May it protect me.
May it protect my teacher.
OM  *Shānti Shānti Shānti*

The Bhagavad Gita
## *The Illumined Man*

ARJUNA:
Tell me of the man who lives in wisdom,
Ever aware of the Self, O Krishna;
How does he talk, how sit, how move about?

SRI KRISHNA:
        He lives in wisdom
Who sees himself in all and all in him,
Whose love for the Lord of Love has consumed
Every selfish desire and sense craving
Tormenting the heart. Not agitated
By grief or hankering after pleasure,
He lives free from lust and fear and anger.
Fettered no more by selfish attachments,
He is not elated by good fortune
Nor depressed by bad. Such is the seer.

Even as a tortoise draws in its limbs
The sage can draw in his senses at will.
An aspirant abstains from sense pleasures,
But he still craves for them. These cravings all
Disappear when he sees the Lord of Love.
For even of one who treads the path
The stormy senses can sweep off the mind.
But he lives in wisdom who subdues them,
And keeps his mind ever absorbed in Me.

When you keep thinking about sense objects,
Attachment comes. Attachment breeds desire,
The lust of possession which, when thwarted,
Burns to anger. Anger clouds the judgment
And robs you of the power to learn from past mistakes.
Lost is the discriminative faculty, and your life
Is utter waste.

But when you move amidst the world of sense
From both attachment and aversion freed,
There comes the peace in which all sorrows end,
And you live in the wisdom of the Self.

The disunited mind is far from wise;
How can it meditate? How be at peace?
When you know no peace, how can you know joy?
When you let your mind follow the siren call
Of the senses, they carry away
Your better judgment as a typhoon drives a boat
Off the charted course to its doom.

Use your mighty arms to free the senses
From attachment and aversion alike,
And live in the full wisdom of the Self.
Such a sage awakes to light in the night
Of all creatures. Wherein they are awake
Is the night of ignorance to the sage.

As the rivers flow into the ocean,
But cannot make the vast ocean o'erflow,
So flow the magic streams of the sense world
Into the sea of peace that is the sage.

He is forever free who has broken out
Of the ego cage of *I* and *mine*
To be united with the Lord of Love.
This is the supreme state. Attain thou this
And pass from death to immortality.

The Jewish Prayer Book
# *The Shema*

*Hear, O Israel,*
* the Lord our God, the Lord is one.*
*Blessed is his name,*
* whose glorious kingdom is forever.*

And thou shalt love the Lord with all your heart,
and with all your soul, and with all your might. And
these words, which I command you this day, shall be
upon your heart: and you shall teach them always
to your children, and shall talk of them when you sit
in your house, when you walk by the way, when
you lie down, and when you arise.

And you shall bind them as a sign on your hand,
and they will be seen as a badge between your eyes.

And you shall write them on the doorposts
of your house, and upon your gates.

Solomon ibn Gabirol
# *Adon Olam*

The Lord of the universe
Ruled before creation.

When by his will all things came to be
The name of the Lord was known.

As the Lord creates, he may end the creation,
Remaining alone, unmanifested.
He was, he is, and he shall remain eternal.

He is without beginning,
He is without end.

He is my God, my living strength,
My refuge when I grieve.
He is my only desire.
I live in him alone.

My soul abides in his hands
In sleep as in wakefulness.

Though I leave my body
I will not fear,
For the Lord is with my soul.

Lao Tzu
# Tao Te Ching

## 52

The universe had a beginning
Called the Mother of All Things.
Once you have found the Mother
You can know her children.
Having known the children,
Hold tightly to the Mother.
Your whole life will be preserved from peril.

Open up the openings,
Multiply your affairs,
Your whole life will become a burden.

He who sees the small is called clear-headed,
He who holds to gentleness is called strong.

Use the light.
Come home to your true nature.
Don't cause yourself injury:
This is known as seizing truth.

## 56

He who knows does not speak,
He who speaks does not know.
Stop up the openings,
Close down the doors,
Rub off the sharp edges.
Unravel all confusion.
Harmonize the light,
Give up contention:
This is called finding the unity of life.

When love and hatred cannot affect you,
Profit and loss cannot touch you,
Praise and blame cannot ruffle you,
You are honored by all the world.

# Prayers from the Rig Veda

## 1

May we be united in heart.
May we be united in speech.
May we be united in mind.
May we perform our duties.
As did the wise men of old.

May we be united in our prayer.
May we be united in our goal.
May we be united in our resolve.
May we be united in our understanding.
May we be united in our offering.
May we be united in our feelings.
May we be united in our hearts.
May we be united in our thoughts.
May there be perfect unity amongst us.

## 2

God makes the rivers to flow. They tire not, nor do they cease from flowing.

May the river of my life flow into the sea of love that is the Lord. May I overcome all the impediments in my course. May the thread of my song be not cut before my life merges in the sea of love.

Guard me against all danger, O Lord. Accept me graciously, O King of kings.

Release me from my sorrows, which hold me as ropes hold a calf. I cannot even open my eyes without the power of your love.

Guard us against the grief that haunts the life of the selfish. Lead us from darkness into light.

We will sing of your love as it was sung of old. Your laws change not, but stand like the mountains.

Forgive me all the mistakes I have committed. Many mornings will dawn upon us again. Guide us through them all, O Lord of Love.

# The Poems of Saint Teresa of Avila

### 1

I gave all my heart to the Lord of Love,
And my life is so completely transformed
That my Beloved One has become mine
And without a doubt I am his at last.

When that tender hunter from paradise
Released his piercing arrow at me,
My wounded soul fell in his loving arms,
And my life is so completely transformed
That my Beloved One has become mine
And without a doubt I am his at last.

He pierced my heart with his arrow of love
And made me one with the Lord who made me.
This is the only love I have to prove.
And my life is so completely transformed
That my Beloved One has become mine
And without a doubt I am his at last.

### 2

Her heart is full of joy with love,
For in the Lord her mind is stilled.
She has renounced every selfish attachment
And draws abiding joy and strength from the One within.
She lives not for herself, but lives
To serve the Lord of Love in all,
And swims across the sea of life
Breasting its rough waves joyfully.

### 3

Let nothing upset you,
Let nothing frighten you.
Everything is changing;
God alone is changeless.
Patience attains the goal.
Who has God lacks nothing;
God alone fills all his needs.

The Chandi
# Hymn to the Divine Mother

O thou the giver of all blessings,
O thou the doer of all good,
O thou the fulfiller of all desires,
O thou the giver of refuge—
Our salutations to thee, O Mother Divine.

O thou Eternal Mother,
Thou hast the power to create, to preserve,
    and to dissolve.
Thou the dwelling-place and embodiment
    of the three gunas—
Our salutations to thee, O Mother Divine.

O thou the savior of all who take refuge in thee,
The lowly and the distressed—
O Mother Divine, we salute thee,
Who takest away the sufferings of all.

# The Dhammapada
## *Twin Verses*

All that we are is the result of what we have thought:
we are formed and molded by our thoughts. The man
whose mind is shaped by selfish thoughts causes misery
when he speaks or acts. Sorrows roll over him as the wheels
of a cart roll over the tracks of the bullock that draws it.

All that we are is the result of what we have thought:
we are formed and molded by our thoughts. The man
whose mind is shaped by selfless thoughts gives joy
whenever he speaks or acts. Joy follows him like a shadow
that never leaves him.

"He insulted me, he struck me, he cheated me, he robbed
me": those caught in resentful thoughts never find peace.

"He insulted me, he struck me, he cheated me, he robbed
me": those who give up resentful thoughts surely find
peace.

For hatred does not cease by hatred at any time: hatred
ceases by love. This is an unalterable law.

There are those who forget that death will come to all.
For those who remember, quarrels come to an end.

He who lives only for pleasure, who eats intemperately,
who is lazy and weak and has no control over his senses,
is like a tree with shallow roots. As a strong wind uproots
such a tree, Mara will throw this man down.

He who lives without looking for pleasures, who eats
temperately and controls his senses, who is persevering
and firm in faith, is like a mountain. As a strong wind
cannot uproot a mountain, Mara cannot throw
this man down.

The deluded, imagining trivial things to be vital to life,
follow their vain fancies and never attain the highest
knowledge.

But the wise, knowing what is trivial and what is vital,
set their thoughts on the supreme goal and attain the
highest knowledge.

As rain seeps through a poorly thatched roof, passion seeps into the untrained mind.

As rain cannot seep through a well-thatched roof, passion cannot seep into a well-trained mind.

Whoever puts on the saffron robe but is self-willed, speaks untruthfully, and lacks self-control, is not worthy of that sacred garment.

But the man who has vanquished self-will, who speaks the truth and has mastered himself, is firmly established on the spiritual path and worthy of the saffron robe.

The selfish man suffers here, and he suffers there; he suffers wherever he goes. He suffers and frets over the damage he has done.

The selfless man rejoices here, and he rejoices there; he rejoices wherever he goes. He rejoices and delights in the good he has done.

The selfish man suffers here, and he suffers there; he suffers wherever he goes. He suffers as he broods over the damage he has done. He suffers more and more as he travels along the path of sorrow.

The selfless man is happy here, and he is happy there; he is happy wherever he goes. He is happy when he thinks of the good he has done. He grows in happiness as he progresses along the path of bliss.

The man who recites many scriptures but fails to practice their teachings is like a cowherd counting another's cows. He does not share in the joys of the spiritual life.

The man who knows few scriptures but practices their teachings, who overcomes all lust, hatred, and delusion, lives with a pure mind in the highest wisdom. He stands without external supports and shares in the joys of the spiritual life.

Thomas a Kempis
# The Wonderful Effects of Divine Love

### 1

Ah, Lord God, thou holy lover of my soul, when thou comest into my heart, all that is within me shall rejoice.

Thou art my glory and the exultation of my heart: Thou art my hope and refuge in the day of my trouble.

### 2

But because I am as yet weak in love, and imperfect in virtue, I have need to be strengthened and comforted by thee; visit me therefore often, and instruct me with all holy discipline.

Set me free from evil passions, and heal my heart of all inordinate affections; that being inwardly cured and thoroughly cleansed, I may be made fit to love, courageous to suffer, steady to persevere.

### 3

Love is a great thing, yea, a great and thorough good; by itself it makes every thing that is heavy, light; and it bears evenly all that is uneven.

For it carries a burden which is no burden, and makes every thing that is bitter, sweet and tasteful.

The noble love of Jesus impels a man to do great things, and stirs him up to be always longing for what is more perfect.

Love desires to be aloft, and will not be kept back by any thing low and mean.

Love desires to be free, and estranged from all worldly affections, that so its inward sight may not be hindered; that it may not be entangled by any temporal prosperity, or by any adversity subdued.

Nothing is sweeter than love, nothing more courageous, nothing higher, nothing wider, nothing more pleasant, nothing fuller nor better in heaven and earth; because love is born of God, and cannot rest but in God, above all created things.

### 4

He that loveth, flyeth, runneth, and rejoiceth; he is free, and cannot be held in.

He giveth all for all, and hath all in all; because he resteth in One highest above all things, from whom all that is good flows and proceeds.

He respecteth not the gifts, but turneth himself above all goods unto the Giver.

Love oftentimes knoweth no measure, but is fervent beyond all measure.

Love feels no burden, thinks nothing of trouble, attempts what is above its strength, pleads no excuse of impossibility; for it thinks all things lawful for itself and all things possible.

It is therefore able to undertake all things, and it completes many things, and warrants them to take effect, where he who does not love, would faint and lie down.

## 5

Love is watchful, and sleeping slumbereth not.

Though weary, it is not tired; though pressed, it is not straitened; though alarmed, it is not confounded; but as a lively flame and burning torch, it forces its way upwards, and securely passes through all.

If any man love, he knoweth what is the cry of this voice. For it is a loud cry in the ears of God, the mere ardent affection of the soul, when it saith, 'My God, my love, thou art all mine, and I am all thine.'

## 6

Enlarge thou me in love, that with the inward palate of my heart I may taste how sweet it is to love, and to be dissolved, and as it were to bathe myself in thy love.

Let me be possessed by love, mounting above myself, through excessive fervour and admiration.

Let me sing the song of love, let me follow thee, my Beloved, on high; let my soul spend itself in thy praise, rejoicing through love.

Let me love thee more than myself, nor love myself but for thee: and in thee all that truly love thee, as the law of love commandeth, shining out from thyself.

## 7

Love is active, sincere, affectionate, pleasant and amiable; courageous, patient, faithful, prudent, long-suffering, manly, and never seeking itself.

For in whatever instance a person seeketh himself, there he falleth from love.

Love is circumspect, humble, and upright: not yielding to softness, or to levity, nor attending to vain things; it is sober, chaste, steady, quiet, and guarded in all the senses.

Love is subject, and obedient to its superiors, to itself mean and despised, unto God devout and thankful, trusting and hoping always in him, even then when God imparteth no relish of sweetness unto it: for without sorrow none liveth in love.

## 8

He that is not prepared to suffer all things, and to stand to the will of his Beloved, is not worthy to be called a lover of God.

A lover ought to embrace willingly all that is hard and distasteful, for the sake of his Beloved; and not to turn away from him for any contrary accidents.

## Canto Two

**YAMA:**

The joy of the Ātman ever abides,
But not what seems pleasant to the senses.
Both these, differing in their purpose, prompt
Man to action. All is well for them who
Choose the joy of the Ātman, but they miss
The goal of life who prefer the pleasant.
Perennial joy or passing pleasure?
This is the choice man is to make always.
The wise man recognizes this, but not
The ignorant. The first welcomes what leads
To abiding joy, though painful at the time.
The latter run, goaded by their senses,
After what seems immediate pleasure.

Well have you renounced these passing pleasures
So dear to the senses, Nachiketa,
And turned your back on the way of the world
Which makes mankind forget the goal of life.

Far apart are wisdom and ignorance:
The first leads man to Self-realization;
The second makes him more and more
Estranged from his real Self. I regard you,
Nachiketa, as worthy of instruction;
For passing pleasures tempt you not at all.

Ignorant of their ignorance, yet wise
In their own esteem, the deluded men
Proud of their vain learning go round and round
Like the blind led by the blind. Far beyond
Their eyes, hypnotized by the world of sense,
Opens the way to immortality.
"I am my body; when my body dies,
I die." Living in this superstition
They fall, life after life, under my sway.

It is but few who hear about the Self.
Fewer still dedicate their lives to its
Realization. Wonderful is the man
Who speaks of the Self. Rare is he
Who makes it the supreme goal of his life.
Blessed is he who, through an illumined
Teacher, attains to Self-realization.
The truth of the Self cannot come through one
Who has not realized that he is the Self.

The intellect can never reach the Self,
Beyond its duality of subject
And object. He who sees himself in all
And all in him helps one through spiritual
Osmosis to realize the Self oneself.
This awakening you have known comes not
Through logic and scholarship, but from
Close association with a realized teacher.
Wise are you, Nachiketa, because you
Seek the Self eternal. May we have more
Seekers like you!

NACHIKETA:

I know that earthly treasures are transient,
And never can I reach the Eternal
Through them. Hence have I renounced
All the desires of Nachiketa for
Earthly treasures to win the Eternal
Through your instruction.

YAMA:

I spread before your eyes, Nachiketa,
The fulfillment of all worldly desires:
Power to dominate the earth, delights
Celestial gained through religious rites, and
Miraculous powers beyond time and space.
These with will and wisdom have you renounced.

The wise, realizing through meditation
The timeless Self, beyond all perception,
Hidden in the cave of the heart,
Leave pleasure and pain far behind.
The man who knows he is neither body
Nor mind, but the immemorial Self,
The divine principle of existence,
Finds the source of all joy and lives in joy
Abiding. I see the gates of joy
Are opening for you, Nachiketa.

NACHIKETA:

Teach me of That you see as beyond right
And wrong, cause and effect, past and future.

YAMA:

I will give you the Word all the scriptures
Glorify, all spiritual disciplines
Express, to attain which aspirants lead
A life of sense-restraint and self-naughting.
It is OM. This symbol of the Godhead
Is the highest. Realizing it one finds
Total fulfillment of all one's longings.

It is of the greatest support to all
Seekers. In whose heart OM reverberates
Unceasingly, he is indeed blessed and
Greatly loved as one who is the Self.

The all-knowing Self was never born,
Nor will it die. Beyond cause and effect,
This Self is eternal and immutable.
When the body dies, the Self does not die.
If the slayer believes that he can kill,
And the slain believes that he can be killed,
Neither knows the truth. The eternal Self
Slays not, nor is ever slain.

Hidden in the heart of every creature
Exists the Self, subtler than the subtlest,
Greater than the greatest. He goes beyond
Sorrow who extinguishes his self-will,
And beholds the glory of the Self through
The grace of the Lord of Love.

Though one sits in meditation in a
Particular place, the Self in him can
Exercise its influence far away.
Though still, it moves everything everywhere.

When the wise man realizes the Self,
Formless in the midst of forms, changeless in
The midst of change, omnipresent and
Supreme, he goes beyond sorrow.

The Self cannot be known through the study
Of the scriptures, nor through the intellect,
Nor through hearing discourses about it.
It can be attained only by him
Whom the Self chooses. Verily unto him
Does the Self reveal itself.

The Self cannot be known by anyone
Who desists not from unrighteous ways,
Controls not his senses, stills not his mind,
And practices not meditation.

None else can know the omnipresent Self,
Whose glory sweeps away the rituals of
The priest and the prowess of the warrior
And puts death itself to death.

## Canto Three

In the secret cave of the heart, two are
Seated by life's fountain. The separate
Ego drinks of the sweet and bitter stuff,
Liking the sweet, disliking the bitter,
While the supreme Self drinks sweet and bitter
Neither liking this nor disliking that.
The ego gropes in darkness, while the Self
Lives in light. So declare the illumined
Sages, and the householders who worship
The sacred fire in the name of the Lord.
May we light the fire of Nachiketa
That burns out the ego, and enables
Man to pass from fearful fragmentation
To fearless fullness in the changeless Whole.

Know the Self as lord of the chariot,
The body as the chariot indeed,
The discriminating intellect as
The charioteer, and the mind as the reins.
The senses, say the wise, are the horses;
Selfish desires are the roads they travel.
When the Self is confused, they point out,
With the body, senses, and mind, he seems
To enjoy pleasure and suffer sorrow.

When a man lacks discrimination and
His mind is undisciplined, his senses
Run hither and thither like wild horses.
But they obey the rein like trained horses
When he has discrimination and his
Mind is one-pointed. The man lacking
Discrimination, with little control
Over his thoughts and far from pure, reaches
Not the pure state of immortality
But wanders from death to death, while he who
Has discrimination, with a still mind
And pure heart, reaches journey's end, never
Again to fall into the jaws of death.
With a discriminating intellect
As charioteer, a disciplined mind as reins,
He attains the supreme goal of life
To be united with the Lord of Love.

The senses derive from objects of sense
Perception, sense objects from mind, mind from
Intellect, and intellect from ego;
Ego from undifferentiated
Consciousness, and consciousness from Brahman.
Brahman is the First Cause and last refuge.
Brahman, the hidden Self in everyone,
Does not shine forth. He is revealed only
To those who keep their mind one-pointed
On the Lord of Love and thus develop
A superconscious manner of knowing.
Meditation empowers them to go
Deeper and deeper into consciousness,
From the world of words to the world of thought,
Then beyond thoughts to wisdom in the Self.

Get up! Wake up! Seek the guidance of an
Illumined teacher and realize the Self.
Sharp like a razor's edge is the path,
The sages say, difficult to traverse.

The supreme Self is beyond name and form,
Beyond the senses, inexhaustible,
Without beginning, without end, beyond
Time, space, and causality, eternal,
Immutable. Those who realize the Self
Are forever free from the jaws of death.

The wise, who gain experiential knowledge
Of this timeless tale of Nachiketa,
Narrated by Death, attain the glory
Of living in spiritual awareness.
They who, full of devotion, recite this
Supreme mystery at a spiritual
Gathering, are fit for eternal life.
They are indeed fit for eternal life.

*Part Two*

Sutta Nipata
# Discourse on Good Will

May all beings be filled with joy and peace.
May all beings everywhere,
The strong and the weak,
The great and the small,
The mean and the powerful,
The short and the long,
The subtle and the gross:

May all beings everywhere,
Seen and unseen,
Dwelling far off or nearby,
Being or waiting to become:
May all be filled with lasting joy.

Let no one deceive another,
Let no one anywhere despise another,
Let no one out of anger or resentment
Wish suffering on anyone at all.

Just as a mother with her own life
Protects her child, her only child, from harm,
So within yourself let grow
A boundless love for all creatures.

Let your love flow outward through the universe,
To its height, its depth, its broad extent,
A limitless love, without hatred or enmity.

Then as you stand or walk,
Sit or lie down,
As long as you are awake,
Strive for this with a one-pointed mind;
Your life will bring heaven to earth.

# Psalms

## 23

The Lord is my shepherd;
    I shall not want.
He maketh me to lie down in green pastures:
    He leadeth me beside the still waters.
He restoreth my soul:
    He leadeth me in the paths of righteousness
    for his name's sake.

Yea, though I walk
    through the valley of the shadow of death,
I will fear no evil:
    for thou art with me;
Thy rod and thy staff they comfort me.

Thou preparest a table before me
    in the presence of mine enemies:
Thou anointest my head with oil;
    my cup runneth over.
Surely goodness and mercy shall follow me
    all the days of my life:
And I will dwell in the house of the Lord
    for ever.

## 24

The earth is the Lord's,
    and the fulness thereof;
the world, and they that dwell therein.
For he hath founded it upon the seas,
    and established it upon the floods.

Who shall ascend into the hill of the Lord? or who shall
stand in his holy place? He that hath clean hands,
and a pure heart; who hath not lifted up his soul
unto vanity, nor sworn deceitfully. He shall receive
the blessing from the Lord, and righteousness from
the God of his salvation. This is the generation
of them that seek him,
    that seek thy face, O Jacob.    *Selah*

Lift up your heads, O ye gates; and be ye lift up,
ye everlasting doors; and the King of glory shall come in.
Who is this King of glory? The Lord strong and mighty,
    the Lord mighty in battle.

Lift up your heads, O ye gates; even lift them up,
ye everlasting doors; and the King of glory shall come in.
Who is this King of glory? The Lord of hosts,
    he is the King of glory.    *Selah*

## 100

Make a joyful noise unto the Lord,
    all ye lands.
Serve the Lord with gladness:
    come before his presence with singing.
Know ye that the Lord he is God:
    it is he that hath made us,
    and not we ourselves;
We are his people,
    and the sheep of his pasture.

Enter into his gates with thanksgiving,
    and into his courts with praise:
Be thankful unto him,
    and bless his name.
For the Lord is good;
    his mercy is everlasting;
And his truth endureth
    to all generations.

Brother Lawrence

# The Practice of the Presence of God

O my God, since thou art with me, and I must now, in obedience to thy commands, apply my mind to these outward things, I beseech thee to grant me the grace to continue in thy presence; and to this end do thou prosper me with thy assistance, receive all my works, and possess all my affections. God knoweth best what is needful for us, and all that he does is for our good. If we knew how much he loves us, we should always be ready to receive equally and with indifference from his hand the sweet and the bitter. All would please that came from him. The sorest afflictions never appear intolerable, except when we see them in the wrong light. When we see them as dispensed by the hand of God, when we know that it is our loving Father who abases and distresses us, our sufferings will lose their bitterness and become even matter of consolation.

Let all our employment be to know God; the more one knows him, the more one desires to know him. And as knowledge is commonly the measure of love, the deeper and more extensive our knowledge shall be, the greater will be our love; and if our love of God were great, we should love him equally in pains and pleasures.

Let us not content ourselves with loving God for the mere sensible favors, how elevated soever, which he has done or may do us. Such favors, though never so great, cannot bring us so near to him as faith does in one simple act. Let us seek him often by faith. He is within us; seek him not elsewhere. If we do love him alone, are we not rude, and do we not deserve blame, if we busy ourselves about trifles which do not please and perhaps offend him? It is to be feared these trifles will one day cost us dear.

Let us begin to be devoted to him in good earnest. Let us cast everything besides out of our hearts. He would possess them alone. Beg this favor of him. If we do what we can on our parts, we shall soon see that change wrought in us which we aspire after.

## Saint Augustine
### *Entering into Joy*

Imagine if all the tumult of the body were to quiet down, along with all our busy thoughts about earth, sea, and air;

if the very world should stop, and the mind cease thinking about itself, go beyond itself, and be quite still;

if all the fantasies that appear in dreams and imagination should cease, and there be no speech, no sign:

Imagine if all things that are perishable grew still — for if we listen they are saying, *We did not make ourselves; He made us who abides forever* — imagine, then, that they should say this and fall silent, listening to the very voice of Him who made them and not to that of his creation;

so that we should hear not his word through the tongues of men, nor the voice of angels, nor the clouds' thunder, nor any symbol, but the very Self which in these things we love, and go beyond ourselves to attain a flash of that eternal wisdom which abides above all things:

And imagine if that moment were to go on and on, leaving behind all other sights and sounds but this one vision which ravishes and absorbs and fixes the beholder in joy; so that the rest of eternal life were like that moment of illumination which leaves us breathless:

Would this not be what is bidden in scripture, *Enter thou into the joy of thy lord* ?

# The Isha Upanishad

The Lord is enshrined in the hearts of all.
The Lord is the supreme reality.
Rejoice in him through renunciation.
Covet nothing. All belongs to the Lord.
Thus working may you live a hundred years.
Thus alone can you work in full freedom.

Those who deny the Self are born again
Blind to the Self, enveloped in darkness,
Utterly devoid of love for the Lord.

The Self is one. Ever still, the Self is
Swifter than thought, swifter than the senses.
Though motionless, he outruns all pursuit.
Without the Self, never could life exist.

The Self seems to move, but is ever still.
He seems far away, but is ever near.
He is within all, and he transcends all.

The man who sees all creatures in himself
And himself in all creatures knows no fear.
The man who sees all creatures in himself
And himself in all creatures knows no grief.
How can the multiplicity of life
Delude the man who sees its unity?

The Self is everywhere. Bright is the Self,
Indivisible, untouched by sin, wise,
Immanent and transcendent. He it is
Who holds the cosmos together.

In dark night live those
For whom the world without alone is real;
In night darker still, for whom the world within
Alone is real. The first leads to a life
Of action, the second of meditation.
But he who combines action with meditation
Goes across the sea of death through action
And enters into immortality
Through the practice of meditation.
So have we heard from the wise.

In dark night live those for whom the Lord
Is transcendent only; in night darker still,
For whom he is immanent only.
But the man for whom he is transcendent
And immanent crosses the sea of death
With the immanent and enters into
Immortality with the transcendent.
So have we heard from the wise.

The face of truth is hidden by your orb
Of gold, O sun. May you remove the orb
So that I, who adore the true, may see
The glory of truth. O nourishing sun,
Solitary traveler, controller,
Source of life for all creatures, spread your light,
And subdue your dazzling splendor
So that I may see your blessed Self.
Even that very Self am I!

May my life merge in the Immortal
When my body is reduced to ashes!
O mind, meditate on the eternal
Brahman. Remember the deeds of the past.
Remember, O mind, remember.

O God of fire, lead us by the good path
To eternal joy. You know all our deeds.
Deliver us from evil, we that bow
And pray again and again.

OM *Shānti Shānti Shānti*

Ansari of Herat

# Invocations

In the name of God,
Most gracious,
Most merciful.

O thou munificent one
Who art the bestower of all bounties,
O thou wise one
Who overlookest our faults,
O self-existent one
Who art beyond our comprehension,
O thou omnipotent one
Who hast no equal in power and greatness,
Who art without a second:
O thou merciful one
Who guidest stray souls to the right path,
Thou art truly our God.

Give purity to our minds,
Aspiration to our hearts,
Light to our eyes.
Out of thy grace and bounty
Give us that which thou deemest best.

O Lord, out of thy grace
Give faith and light to our hearts,
And with the medicine of truth and steadfastness
Cure the ills of our life.
I know not what to ask of thee.
Thou art the knower;
Give what thou deemest best.

O God, may my brain reel with thoughts of thee,
May my heart thrill with the mysteries of thy grace,
May my tongue move only to utter thy praise.

I live only to do thy will,
My lips move only in praise of thee,
O Lord, whoever becometh aware of thee
Casteth out all else other than thee.

O Lord, give me a heart
That I may pour it out in thanksgiving.
Give me life
That I may spend it in working
For the salvation of the world.

O Lord, give me that right discrimination
That the lure of the world may cheat me no more.
Give me strength
That my faith suffer no eclipse.

O Lord, give me understanding
That I stray not from the path.
Give me light
To avoid pitfalls.

O Lord, keep watch over me
That I stray not.
Keep me on the path of righteousness
That I escape from the pangs of repentance.

O Lord, judge me not by my actions.
Of thy mercy, save me,
And make my humble efforts fruitful.

O Lord, give me a heart
Free from the flames of desire.
Give me a mind
Free from the waves of egoism.

O Lord, give me eyes
Which see nothing but thy glory.
Give me a mind
That finds delight in thy service.
Give me a soul
Drunk in the wine of thy wisdom.

O Lord, to find thee is my desire,
But to comprehend thee is beyond my strength.
Remembering thee is solace to my sorrowing heart,
Thoughts of thee are my constant companions.
I call upon thee night and day.
The flame of thy love glows
In the darkness of my night.

Life in my body pulsates only for thee,
My heart beats in resignation to thy will.
If on my dust a tuft of grass were to grow,
Every blade would tremble with my devotion for thee.

O Lord, everyone desires to behold thee.
I desire that thou mayest cast a glance at me.
Let me not disgrace myself.
If thy forgiveness awaits me in the end,
Lower not the standard of forgiveness
Which thou hast unfurled.

O Lord, prayer at thy gate
Is a mere formality:
Thou knowest what thy slave desires.

O Lord, better for me to be dust
And my name effaced
From the records of the world
Than that thou forget me.

He knoweth all our good and evil.
Nothing is hidden from him.
He knoweth what is the best medicine
To cure the pain and to rescue the fallen.
Be humble, for he exalteth the humble.

I am intoxicated with love for thee
And need no fermented wine.
I am thy bird, free from need of seed
And safe from the snare of the fowler.
In the kaaba and in the temple
Thou art the object of my search.
Else I am freed
From both these places of worship.

Lord, when thou wert hidden from me
The fever of life possessed me.
When thou revealest thyself
This fever of life departeth.

O Lord, other men are afraid of thee
But I — I am afraid of myself.
From thee flows good alone,
From me flows evil.
Others fear what the morrow may bring.
I am afraid of what happened yesterday.

O Lord, if thou holdest me responsible for my sins
I shall cling to thee for thy grace.
I with my sin am an insignificant atom.
Thy grace is resplendent as the sun.

O Lord, out of regard for thy name,
The qualities which are thine,
Out of regard for thy greatness,
Listen to my cry,
For thou alone canst redeem me.

O Lord, intoxicate me with the wine of thy love.
Place the chains of thy slavery on my feet;
Make me empty of all but thy love,
And in it destroy me and bring me back to life.
The hunger thou hast awakened
Culminates in fulfillment.

Make my body impervious to the fires of hell;
Vouchsafe to me a vision of thee in heaven.
The spark thou hast kindled, make it everlasting.

I think of no other,
And in thy love care for none else.
None has a place in my heart but thee.
My heart has become thy abode;
It has no place for another.

O Lord, thou cherishest the helpless
And I am helpless.
Apply thy balm to my bleeding heart,
For thou art the physician.

O Lord, I, a beggar, ask of thee
More than what a thousand kings may ask of thee.
Each one has something he needs to ask of thee.
I have come to ask thee to give me thyself.

If words can establish a claim,
I claim a crown.
But if deeds are wanted,
I am as helpless as the ant.

Urged by desire, I wandered
In the streets of good and evil.
I gained nothing except feeding the fire of desire.
As long as in me remains the breath of life,
Help me, for thou alone canst hear my prayer.

Watch vigilantly the state of thine own mind.
Love of God begins in harmlessness.

Know that the Prophet built an external kaaba
Of clay and water,
And an inner kaaba in life and heart.
The outer kaaba was built by Abraham, the holy;
The inner is sanctified by the glory of God himself.

On the path of God
Two places of worship mark the stages,
The material temple
And the temple of the heart.
Make your best endeavor
To worship at the temple of the heart.

In this path, be a man
With a heart full of compassion.
Engage not in vain doing;
Make not thy home in the street of lust and desire.

If thou wouldst become a pilgrim on the path of love,
The first condition is that thou become
As humble as dust and ashes.

Know that when thou learnest to lose thy self
Thou wilt reach the Beloved.
There is no other secret to be revealed,
And more than this is not known to me.

Be humble and cultivate silence.
If thou hast received, rejoice,
And fill thyself with ecstasy.
And if not, continue the demand.

What is worship?
To realize reality.
What is the sacred law?
To do no evil.
What is reality?
Selflessness.

The heart enquired of the soul,
What is the beginning of this business?
What its end, and what its fruit?
The soul answered:
The beginning of it is the annihilation of self,
Its end faithfulness,
And its fruit immortality.

The heart asked, what is annihilation?
What is faithfulness?
What is immortality?
The soul answered:
Freedom from self is annihilation.
Faithfulness is fulfillment of love.
Immortality is the union of immortal with mortal.

In this path the eye must cease to see
And the ear to hear,
Save unto Him and about Him.
Be as dust on his path;
Even the kings of this earth
Make the dust of his feet
The balm of their eyes.

Thomas a Kempis
## *Four Things That Bring Much Inward Peace*

—My son, now will I teach thee the way of peace
  and true liberty.
—O Lord, I beseech thee, do as thou sayest, for this
  is delightful to me to hear.

—Be desirous, my son, to work for the welfare of another
    rather than seek thine own will.
  Choose always to have less
    rather than more.
  Seek always the lowest place,
    and to be inferior to everyone.
  Wish always, and pray, that the will of God
    may be wholly fulfilled in thee.
  Behold, such a man
    entereth within the borders of peace and rest.

—O Lord, this short discourse of thine containeth
  within itself much perfection. It is little to be spoken,
  but full of meaning, and abundant in fruit. . . . Thou
  who canst do all things, and ever lovest the profiting
  of my soul, increase in me thy grace, that I may be able
  to fulfill thy words, and to work out mine own
  salvation.

Swami Ramdas

# The Central Truth

Forget not the central truth that God
is seated in your own heart. Don't be
disheartened by failures at initial stages.
Cultivate the spirit of surrender to the
workings of his will, inside you and outside
you, until you have completely surrendered
up your ego-sense and have known that
he is in all, and he is all, and you and he are
one. Be patient. The path of self-discipline
that leads to God-realization is not an
easy path: obstacles and sufferings are on
the path; the latter you must bear, and
the former overcome — all by his help.
His help comes only through concentration. Repetition of God's name helps
concentration.

Sri Sarada Devi
## The Whole World Is Your Own

I tell you one thing —
If you want peace of mind,
    do not find fault with others.
Rather learn to see your own faults.
Learn to make the whole world your own.
No one is a stranger, my child;
    this whole world is your own.

Mahatma Gandhi
## The Path

I know the path: it is strait and narrow.
It is like the edge of a sword. I rejoice to
walk on it. I weep when I slip. God's
word is: "He who strives never perishes."
I have implicit faith in that promise.
Though, therefore, from my weakness
I fail a thousand times, I shall not
lose faith.

Seng Ts'an
# Believing in Mind

The great Way has no impediments,
It does not pick and choose.
When you abandon attachment and aversion
You see it plainly.
Make a thousandth of an inch distinction,
Heaven and earth swing apart.
If you want it to appear before your eyes
Cherish neither 'for' nor 'against'.

To compare what you like with what you dislike,
That is the disease of the mind.
You pass over the hidden meaning,
Peace of mind is needlessly troubled.

It is round and perfect like vast space,
Lacks nothing, never overflows.
Only because we take and reject
Do we lose the means to know its Suchness.

Don't get tangled in outward desire
Or get caught within yourself.
Once you plant deep the longing for peace
Confusion leaves of itself.

Return to the root and you find meaning;
Follow sense objects, you lose the goal.
Just one instant of inner enlightenment
Will take you far beyond the emptiness of the world.

Selfish attachment forgets all limits;
It always leads down evil roads.
When you let go of it, things happen of themselves;
The substance neither goes nor abides.

If the eye does not sleep
All dreams will naturally stop.
If the mind does not differentiate
All things are of one Suchness.

When you fathom the nature of Suchness
You instantly forget all selfish desire.
Having seen ten thousand things as one
You return to your natural state.

Without meditation
Consciousness and feeling are hard to grasp.
In the realm of Suchness
There is neither self nor other.

In the one there is the all,
In the all, there is the one.
If you know this,
You will never worry about being incomplete.

If belief and mind are made the same
And there is no division between belief and mind
The road of words comes to an end,
Beyond present and future.

# The Bhagavad Gita
## *The Way of Love*

ARJUNA:

Of those who love you as the Lord of Love,
Ever present in all, and those who seek you
As the nameless, formless Reality,
Which way is sure and swift, love or knowledge?

SRI KRISHNA:

For those who set their hearts on Me
And worship Me with unfailing devotion and faith,
The way of love leads sure and swift to Me.

Those who seek the transcendental Reality,
Unmanifested, without name or form,
Beyond the reach of feeling and of thought,
With their senses subdued and mind serene
And striving for the good of all beings,
They too will verily come unto Me.

Yet hazardous and slow is the path to the Unrevealed,
Difficult for physical man to tread.
But they for whom I am the goal supreme,
Who do all work renouncing self for Me
And meditate on Me with single-hearted devotion,
These will I swiftly rescue
From the fragment's cycle of birth and death
To fullness of eternal life in Me.

Still your mind in Me, still yourself in Me,
And without doubt you shall be united with Me,
Lord of Love, dwelling in your heart.
But if you cannot still your mind in Me,
Learn to do so through the practice of meditation.
If you lack the will for such self-discipline,
Engage yourself in selfless service of all around you,
For selfless service can lead you at last to Me.
If you are unable to do even this,
Surrender yourself to Me in love,
Receiving success and failure with equal calmness
As granted by Me.

Better indeed is knowledge than mechanical practice.
Better than knowledge is meditation.
But better still is surrender in love,
Because there follows immediate peace.

That one I love who is incapable of ill will,
And returns love for hatred.
Living beyond the reach of 'I and mine'
And of pleasure and pain, full of mercy,
Contented, self-controlled, firm in faith,
With all his heart and all his mind given to Me—
With such a one I am in love.

Not agitating the world or by it agitated,
He stands above the sway of elation,
Competition, and fear, accepting life
Good and bad as it comes. He is pure,
Efficient, detached, ready to meet every demand
I make on him as a humble instrument of My work.

He is dear to Me who runs not after the pleasant
Or away from the painful, grieves not
Over the past, lusts not today,
But lets things come and go as they happen.

Who serves both friend and foe with equal love,
Not buoyed up by praise or cast down by blame,
Alike in heat and cold, pleasure and pain,
Free from selfish attachments and self-will,
Ever full, in harmony everywhere,
Firm in faith — such a one is dear to Me.

But dearest to Me are those who seek Me
In faith and love as life's eternal goal.
They go beyond death to immortality.

Saint Matthew
# *The Sermon on the Mount*

## 1

Blessed are the poor in spirit:
>for theirs is the kingdom of heaven.

Blessed are they that mourn:
>for they shall be comforted.

Blessed are the meek:
>for they shall inherit the earth.

Blessed are they which do hunger and thirst
after righteousness:
>for they shall be filled.

Blessed are the merciful:
>for they shall obtain mercy.

Blessed are the pure in heart:
>for they shall see God.

Blessed are they which are persecuted
for righteousness' sake:
>for theirs is the kingdom of heaven.

Blessed are the peacemakers:
>for they shall be called the children of God.

Blessed are ye, when men shall revile you, and persecute you, and shall say all manner of evil against you falsely, for my sake. Rejoice, and be exceeding glad: for great is your reward in heaven: for so persecuted they the prophets which were before you.

Ye are the salt of the earth: but if the salt have lost his savour, wherewith shall it be salted? It is thenceforth good for nothing, but to be cast out, and to be trodden under foot of men.

Ye are the light of the world. A city that is set on an hill cannot be hid. Neither do men light a candle, and put it under a bushel, but on a candlestick; and it giveth light unto all that are in the house. Let your light so shine before men, that they may see your good works, and glorify your Father which is in heaven.

## 2

Ye have heard that it hath been said,
Thou shalt love thy neighbour, and hate thine enemy.
But I say unto you,
    Love your enemies, bless them that curse you,
do good to them that hate you, and pray for them which
despitefully use you, and persecute you; that ye may be
the children of your Father which is in heaven: for he
maketh his sun to rise on the evil and on the good,
and sendeth rain on the just and on the unjust.

For if ye love them which love you, what reward have ye?
Do not even the publicans the same?
And if ye salute your brethren only, what do ye more
than others? Do not even the publicans so?

Be ye therefore perfect,
    even as your Father which is in heaven is perfect.

## 3

Our Father which art in heaven, hallowed be thy name.
Thy kingdom come.
Thy will be done in earth, as it is in heaven.
Give us this day our daily bread,
And forgive us our debts, as we forgive our debtors.
And lead us not into temptation, but deliver us from evil:
For thine is the kingdom,
    and the power, and the glory, for ever.
Amen.

Part Three

Saint Patrick
## *Christ Be with Me*

May the strength of God pilot me,
    the power of God preserve me today.
May the wisdom of God instruct me,
    the eye of God watch over me,
    the ear of God hear me,
    the word of God give me sweet talk,
    the hand of God defend me,
    the way of God guide me.

Christ be with me.
Christ before me.
Christ after me.
Christ in me.
Christ under me.
Christ over me.
Christ on my right hand.
Christ on my left hand.
Christ on this side.
Christ on that side.
Christ at my back.

Christ in the head of everyone
    to whom I speak.
Christ in the mouth of every person
    who speaks to me.
Christ in the eye of every person
    who looks at me.
Christ in the ear of every person
    who hears me today.

The Dhammapada
# *The Brahmin*

Cross the river bravely,
Conquer all your passions,
Go beyond the world of fragments,
And know the deathless Ground of life.

Cross the river bravely,
Conquer all your passions,
Go beyond your likes and dislikes,
And all fetters will fall away.

Who is a true brahmin?
Him I call a brahmin
Who has neither likes nor dislikes,
And is free from the chains of fear.

Who is a true brahmin?
Him I call a brahmin
Who has trained his mind to be still
And reached the supreme goal of life.

Him I call a brahmin
Who does not hurt others
With unkind acts, words, or thoughts.
His body and mind obey him.

Him I call a brahmin
Who walks in the footsteps
Of the Buddha. Light your torch too
From the fire of his sacrifice.

Not matted hair nor birth
Makes a man a brahmin,
But the truth and love for all life
With which his heart is full.

Of what use is matted hair?
Of what use a skin of deer
On which to sit in meditation,
If your mind is seething with lust?

The sun shines in the day;
In the night, the moon;
The warrior shines in battle;
In meditation, the brahmin.
But day and night the Buddha shines
In radiance of love for all.

Him I call a brahmin
Who has shed all evil.
He is called *samana,* 'the serene,'
And *pabbajita,* 'a pure one.'

Him I call a brahmin
Who is never angry,
Never causes harm to others
Even when he is harmed by them.

Him I call a brahmin
Who clings not to pleasure.
Do not cause sorrow to others:
No more sorrow will come to you.

Saffron robe, outward show,
Does not make a brahmin,
But training of the mind and senses
Through practice of meditation.

Not riches nor high caste
Makes a man a brahmin.
Free yourself from selfish desires,
And you will become a brahmin.

He has thrown off his chains;
He trembles not in fear.
No selfish bonds can ensnare him,
No impure thought pollute his mind.

Him I call a brahmin
Who fears not jail nor death.
He has the power of love
No army can defeat.

Him I call a brahmin
Who clings not to pleasure,
Like water on a lotus leaf,
Or mustard seed on a needle.

Him I call a brahmin
Ever true, ever kind.
He never asks what life can give,
But 'What can I give life?'

Him I call a brahmin
Who has found his heaven,
Free from every selfish desire,
Free from every impurity.

For him no more sorrow will come.
On him no more burden will fall.

Him I call a brahmin
Who has risen above
The duality of this world,
Free from sorrow and free from sin.
He shines like the full moon
With no cloud in the sky.

Him I call a brahmin
Who has crossed the river
Difficult, dangerous to cross,
And safely reached the other shore.

Wanting nothing at all,
Doubting nothing at all,
Master of his body and mind,
He has gone beyond time and death.

Him I call a brahmin
Who turns his back on himself.
Homeless, he is ever at home;
Egoless, he is ever full.

Him I call a brahmin
Who is free from bondage
To human beings and nature,
The hero who has conquered the world.

Self-will has left his mind;
It will never return.
Sorrow has left his life;
It will never return.

Him I call a brahmin
Free from *I, me,* and *mine*
Who knows the rise and fall of life.
He will not fall asleep again.

Him I call a brahmin
Whose way no one can know.
He lives free from past and future;
He lives free from decay and death.

Possessing nothing, desiring nothing
For his own pleasure, his own profit,
He has become a force for good,
Working for the freedom of all.

He has reached the end of the way;
He has crossed the river of life.
All that he had to do is done;
He has become one with all life.

## The Bhagavad Gita
# *Whatever You Do*

A leaf, a flower, a fruit, or even
Water, offered to Me in devotion,
I will accept as the loving gift
Of a dedicated heart. Whatever you do,
Make it an offering to Me —
The food you eat or worship you perform,
The help you give, even your suffering.
Thus will you be free from karma's bondage,
From the results of action, good and bad.

I am the same to all beings. My love
Is the same always. Nevertheless, those
Who meditate on Me with devotion,
They dwell in Me, and I shine forth in them.

Even the worst sinner becomes a saint
When he loves Me with all his heart. This love
Will soon transform his personality
And fill his heart with peace profound.
O son of Kunti, this is my promise:
The man who loves Me, he shall never perish.

Even those who are handicapped by birth
Have reached the supreme goal of life,
By taking refuge in Me. How much more
The pure brahmins and royal sages who love Me!

Give not your love to this transient world
Of suffering, but give all your love to Me.
Give Me your mind, your heart, all your worship.
Long for Me always, live for Me always,
And you shall be united with Me.

# The Kena Upanishad

## Canto One

The student inquires: "Who makes my mind think?
Who fills my body with vitality?
Who causes my tongue to speak? Who is that
Invisible One who sees through my eyes
And hears through my ears?"

The teacher replies: "The Self is the ear of the ear,
The eye of the eye, the mind of the mind,
The word of words, and the life of life.
Rising above the senses and the mind
And renouncing separate existence,
The wise realize the deathless Self.

"Him our eyes cannot see, nor words express;
He cannot be grasped even by our mind.
We do not know, we cannot understand,
Because he is different from the known,
And he is different from the unknown.
Thus have we heard from the illumined ones.

"That which makes the tongue speak, but cannot be
Spoken by the tongue, know that as the Self.
This Self is not someone other than you.

"That which makes the mind think, but cannot be
Thought by the mind, that is the Self indeed.
This Self is not someone other than you.

"That which makes the eye see, but cannot be
Seen by the eye, that is the Self indeed.
This Self is not someone other than you.

"That which makes the ear hear, but cannot be
Heard by the ear, that is the Self indeed.
This Self is not someone other than you.

"That which makes you draw breath, but cannot be
Drawn by your breath, that is the Self indeed.
This Self is not someone other than you."

# Poems of Kabir

## 1

O Sadhu, the simple union is the best.
Since the day when I met with my Lord,
There has been no end to the sport of our love.
I shut not my eyes, I close not my ears,
I do not mortify my body; I see with eyes open
And smile and behold his beauty everywhere:
I utter his name, and whatever I see,
It reminds me of him; whatever I do,
It becomes his worship.
The rising and the setting are one to me:
All contradictions are solved.
Wherever I go, I move round him.
All I achieve is his service: when I lie down,
I lie prostrate at his feet.
He is the only adorable One to me:
I have none other. My tongue has left off impure words,
It sings his glory, day and night.
Whether I rise or sit down, I can never forget him,
For the rhythm of his music beats in my ears.
Kabir says: My heart is frenzied
And I disclose in my soul what is hidden.
I am immersed in that great bliss
Which transcends all pleasure and pain.

## 2

The Lord is in me, the Lord is in you,
    as life is in every seed.
O servant! Put false pride away, and seek for him
    within you.
A million suns are ablaze with light,
The sea of blue spreads in the sky,
The fever of life is stilled, and all stains
    are washed away
When I sit in the midst of that world.

Hark to the unstruck bells and drums!
Take your delight in love!
Rains pour down without water, and the rivers
    are streams of light.
One love it is that pervades the whole world,
    few there are who know it fully:
They are blind who hope to see it by the light of reason,
    that reason which is the cause of separation —
The House of Reason is very far away!

How blessed is Kabir, that amidst this great joy he sings
    within his own vessel.
It is the music of the meeting of soul with soul;
It is the music of the forgetting of sorrows;
It is the music that transcends all coming in
    and all going forth.

Thomas a Kempis
# Lord That Giveth Strength

## 1

My son, I am the Lord, that giveth strength in the day of tribulation.

Come thou unto Me, when it is not well with thee.

This is that which most of all hindereth heavenly consolation, that thou art too slow in turning thyself unto prayer.

For before thou dost earnestly supplicate Me, thou seekest in the meanwhile many comforts, and refreshest thyself in outward things.

And hence it comes to pass that all doth little profit thee, until thou well consider that I am he who do rescue them that trust in Me; and that out of Me, there is neither powerful help, nor profitable counsel, nor lasting remedy.

But do thou, having now recovered breath after the tempest, gather strength again in the light of my mercies; for I am at hand (saith the Lord) to repair all, not only entirely, but also abundantly and in most plentiful measure.

## 2

Is there any thing hard to Me? or shall I be like one that saith and doeth not?

Where is thy faith? stand firmly and with perseverance; take courage and be patient; comfort will come to thee in due time.

Wait, wait I say, for Me: I will come and take care of thee.

It is a temptation that vexeth thee, and a vain fear that affrighteth thee.

What else doth anxiety about future contingencies bring thee, but sorrow upon sorrow? 'Sufficient for the day is the evil thereof.'

It is a vain thing and unprofitable, to be either disturbed or pleased about future things, which perhaps will never come to pass.

## 3

But it is incident to man, to be deluded with such imaginations; and a sign of a mind as yet weak, to be so easily drawn away by the suggestions of the Enemy.

For so he may delude and deceive thee, he careth not whether it be by true or by false propositions; nor whether he overthrows thee with the love of present, or the fear of future things.

Let not therefore thy heart be troubled, neither let it fear.

Trust in Me, and put thy confidence in my mercy.

When thou thinkest thyself farthest off from Me, often-times I am nearest unto thee.

When thou countest almost all to be lost, then oftentimes the greatest gain of reward is close at hand.

All is not lost, when any thing falleth out contrary.

Thou oughtest not to judge according to present feeling; nor so to take any grief, or give thyself over to it, from whencesoever it cometh, as though all hopes of escape were quite taken away.

## 4

Think not thyself wholly left, although for a time I have sent thee some tribulation, or even have withdrawn thy desired comfort; for this is the way to the kingdom of heaven.

And without doubt it is more expedient for thee and the rest of my servants, that ye be exercised with adversities, than that ye should have all things according to your desires.

I know the secret thoughts of thy heart, and that it is very expedient for thy welfare, that thou be left sometimes without taste [of spiritual sweetness, and in a dry condition], lest perhaps thou shouldest be puffed up with thy prosperous estate, and shouldest be willing to please thyself in that which thou art not.

That which I have given, I can take away; and I can restore it again when I please.

## 5

When I give it, it is mine; when I withdraw it, I take not any thing that is thine; for mine is every good gift and every perfect gift.

If I send upon thee affliction, or any cross whatever, repine not, nor let thy heart fail thee; I can quickly succour thee, and turn all thy heaviness into joy.

Howbeit I am righteous, and greatly to be praised when I deal thus with thee.

## 6

If thou art wise, and considerest what the truth is, thou never oughtest to mourn dejectedly for any adversity that befalleth thee, but rather to rejoice and give thanks.

Yea, thou wilt account this time especial joy, that I afflict thee with sorrows, and do not spare thee.

'As the Father hath loved Me, I also love you,' said I unto My beloved disciples; whom certainly I sent not out to temporal joys, but to great conflicts; not to honours, but to contempts; not to idleness, but to labours; not to rest, but to bring forth much fruit with patience. Remember thou these words, O my son!

# Songs of Sri Ramakrishna

## 1

Dwell, O mind, within yourself;
Enter no other's home.
If you but seek there, you will find
All you are searching for.

God, the true Philosopher's Stone,
Who answers every prayer,
Lies hidden deep within your heart,
The richest gem of all.

How many pearls and precious stones
Are scattered all about
The outer court that lies before
The chamber of your heart!

## 2

Oh, when will dawn for me that day of blessedness
When He who is all Good, all Beauty, and all Truth
Will light the inmost shrine of my heart?
When shall I sink at last, ever beholding Him,
Into that Ocean of Delight?
Lord, as Infinite Wisdom Thou shalt enter my soul,
And my unquiet mind, made speechless by Thy sight,
Will find a haven at Thy feet.
In my heart's firmament, O Lord, Thou wilt arise
As Blissful Immortality; and as, when the chakora
Beholds the rising moon, it sports about for very joy,
So, too, shall I be filled with heavenly happiness
When Thou appearest unto me.

Thou One without a Second, all Peace, the King of Kings!
At Thy beloved feet I shall renounce my life
And so at last shall gain life's goal;
I shall enjoy the bliss of heaven while yet on earth!
Where else is a boon so rare bestowed?
Then shall I see Thy glory, pure and untouched by stain;
As darkness flees from light, so will my darkest sins
Desert me at Thy dawn's approach. Kindle in me, O Lord,
The blazing fire of faith to be the pole-star of my life;
O Succour of the weak, fulfil my one desire!
Then shall I bathe both day and night
In the boundless bliss of Thy Love, and utterly forget
Myself, O Lord, attaining Thee.

## 3

I have joined my heart to Thee:
 all that exists art Thou;
Thee only have I found, for Thou art all that exists.
O Lord, Beloved of my heart!
 Thou art the Home of all;
Where indeed is the heart in which Thou dost not dwell?
Thou hast entered every heart:
 all that exists art Thou.
Whether sage or fool, whether Hindu or Mussalmān,
Thou makes them as Thou wilt:
 all that exists art Thou.

Thy presence is everywhere,
 whether in heaven or in Kaabā;
Before Thee all must bow, for Thou art all that exists.
From earth below to the highest heaven,
 from heaven to deepest earth,
I see Thee wherever I look: all that exists art Thou.
Pondering, I have understood;
 I have seen it beyond a doubt;
I find not a single thing that may be compared to Thee.
To Jāfar it has been revealed
 that Thou art all that exists.

## 4

Thou art my All in All, O Lord — the Life of my life,
 the Essence of essence;
In the three worlds I have none else but Thee
 to call my own.
Thou art my peace, my joy, my hope; Thou my support,
 my wealth, my glory;
Thou my wisdom and my strength.

Thou art my home, my place of rest; my dearest friend,
 my next of kin;
My present and my future, Thou; my heaven
 and my salvation.
Thou art my scriptures, my commandments;
 Thou art my ever gracious Guru;
Thou the Spring of my boundless bliss.

Thou art the Way and Thou the Goal;
 Thou the Adorable One, O Lord!
Thou art the Mother tender-hearted;
 Thou the chastising Father;
Thou the Creator and Protector;
 Thou the Helmsman who dost steer
My craft across the sea of life.

# The Shvetashvatara Upanishad

## Canto One

Spiritual aspirants ask their teacher:
What is the cause of the cosmos? Is it Brahman?
From where do we come? By what live?
Where shall we find peace at last?
What power governs the duality
Of pleasure and pain by which we are driven?

Time, nature, necessity, accident,
Elements, energy, intelligence —
None of these can be the First Cause.
They are effects, whose only purpose is
To help the self to rise above pleasure and pain.

In the depths of meditation, sages
Saw within themselves the Lord of Love,
Who dwells in the heart of every creature.
Deep in the hearts of all he dwells, hidden
Behind the gunas of law, energy,
And inertia. He is One. He it is
Who rules over time, space, and causality.

The world is the wheel of God, turning round
And round with all living creatures upon
The wheel. The world is the river of God,
Flowing from him and flowing back to him.

On this ever-revolving wheel of life
The individual self goes round and round
Through life after life, believing itself
To be a separate creature, until
It sees its identity with the Lord
Of Love and attains immortality
In the indivisible Whole.

He is the eternal Reality, sing
The scriptures, and the ground of existence.
They who perceive him in every creature
Merge in him and are released from the wheel
Of birth and death.

The Lord of Love holds in his hand the world,
Composed of the changing and the changeless,
The manifest and the unmanifest.
The individual self, not yet aware
Of the Lord, goes after pleasure, to become
Bound more and more. When it sees the Lord,
There comes the end of its bondage.

Conscious spirit and unconscious matter
Both have existed since the dawn of time,
With Maya appearing to connect them,
Misrepresenting joy as eternal.
When all these three are seen as one, the Self
Reveals its universal form and serves
As an instrument of the divine will.

All is change in the world of the senses,
But changeless is the supreme Lord of Love.
Meditate on him, be absorbed in him,
Wake up from this dream of separateness.

Know God and all fetters will fall away.
No longer identifying yourself
With the body, go beyond birth and death.
All your desires will be fulfilled in him
Who is One without a second.

Know him to be enshrined within your heart
Always. Truly there is nothing more to know
In life. Meditate and realize
The world is filled with the presence of God.

Fire is not seen until one firestick rubs
Against another, though the fire remains
Hidden in the firestick. So does the Lord
Remain hidden in the body until
He is revealed through the mystic mantram.

Let your body be the lower firestick;
Let the mantram be the upper. Rub them
Against each other in meditation
And realize the Lord.

Like oil in sesame seeds, like butter
In cream, like water in springs, like fire
In a firestick, so dwells the Lord of Love,
The Self, in the very depths of consciousness.
Realize him through truth and meditation.

The Self is hidden in the hearts of all,
As butter lies hidden in cream. Realize
The Self in the depths of meditation,
The Lord of Love, supreme Reality,
Who is the goal of all knowledge.

This is the highest mystical teaching;
This is the highest mystical teaching.

## Canto Two

May we harness body and mind to see
The Lord of Life who dwells in everyone.
May we with one-pointed mind
Ever strive for blissful union with the Lord.
May our senses through meditation be
Trained to serve the Lord of Life.

Great is the glory of the Lord of Life,
Infinite, omnipresent, all-knowing.
He is known by the wise who meditate
And conserve their vital energy.

Hear, O children of immortal bliss,
You are born to be united with the Lord.
Follow the path of the illumined ones,
And be united with the Lord of Life.

Ignite kundalinī in the depths of
Meditation. Bring your breathing and mind
Under control. Drink deep of divine love,
And you will attain the unitive state.

Dedicate yourself to the Lord of Life,
Who is the cause of the cosmos. He will
Remove the cause of all your suffering
And free you from the bondage of karma.

Be seated with spinal column erect
And deep inwards turn the senses and mind.
With the mantram reverberating in
Your mind, cross the dread sea of birth and death.

Train the senses to be obedient.
Regulate your activities to lead you
To the goal. Hold the reins of your mind
As you hold the reins of restive horses.

Choose a place for meditation that is
Clean, quiet, and cool, a cave with a smooth floor
Without stones and dust, protected against
Wind and rain and pleasing to the eye.

In deep meditation the aspirant
May see forms like snow or smoke. He may feel
A strong wind blowing or a wave of heat.
He may see within him more and more light,
Fireflies, lightning, sun, or moon. These are signs
That he is well on his way to Brahman.

Health, a light body, freedom from cravings,
Clear skin, sonorous voice, a pleasant odor:
These are signs of progress in meditation.

As a dusty mirror shines bright when cleansed,
So shines the man who realizes the Self,
Attains life's goal, and passes beyond sorrow.

In the supreme climax of samādhi
He realizes the presence of the Lord
In his consciousness and is freed from all
Impurities — he the pure and deathless.

The Lord dwells in the womb of the cosmos,
The Creator who is in all creatures.
He is that which is born and to be born;
His face is everywhere.

Let us adore the Lord of Life, who is
Present in fire and water, plants and trees.
Let us adore the Lord of Life!
Let us adore the Lord of Life!

# Saint Paul
## *Epistle on Love*

Though I speak with the tongues of men and of angels, and have not charity, I am become as sounding brass, or a tinkling cymbal. And though I have the gift of prophecy, and understand all mysteries, and all knowledge; and though I have all faith, so that I could remove mountains, and have not charity, I am nothing. And though I bestow all my goods to feed the poor, and though I give my body to be burned, and have not charity, it profiteth me nothing.

Charity suffereth long, and is kind; charity envieth not; charity vaunteth not itself, is not puffed up; doth not behave itself unseemly; seeketh not her own, is not easily provoked, thinketh no evil; rejoiceth not in iniquity, but rejoiceth in the truth; beareth all things, believeth all things, hopeth all things, endureth all things.

Charity never faileth: but whether there be prophecies, they shall fail; whether there be tongues, they shall cease; whether there be knowledge, it shall vanish away. For we know in part, and we prophesy in part. But when that which is perfect is come, then that which is in part shall be done away.

When I was a child, I spake as a child, I understood as a child, I thought as a child: but when I became a man, I put away childish things. For now we see through a glass, darkly; but then face to face: now I know in part; but then shall I know even as also I am known.

And now abideth faith, hope, charity, these three; but the greatest of these is charity.

*—King James Version*

If I speak in the tongues of men and of angels, but have not love, I am a noisy gong or a clanging cymbal. And if I have prophetic powers, and understand all mysteries and all knowledge, and if I have all faith, so as to remove mountains, but have not love, I am nothing. If I give away all I have, and if I deliver my body to be burned, but have not love, I gain nothing.

Love is patient and kind; love is not jealous or boastful; it is not arrogant or rude. Love does not insist on its own way; it is not irritable or resentful; it does not rejoice at wrong, but rejoices in the right. Love bears all things, believes all things, hopes all things, endures all things.

Love never ends; as for prophecies, they will pass away; as for tongues, they will cease; as for knowledge, it will pass away. For our knowledge is imperfect and our prophecy is imperfect; but when the perfect comes, the imperfect will pass away.

When I was a child, I spoke like a child, I thought like a child, I reasoned like a child; when I became a man, I gave up childish ways. For now we see in a mirror dimly, but then face to face. Now I know in part; then I shall understand fully, even as I have been fully understood.

So faith, hope, love abide, these three; but the greatest of these is love.

*—Revised Standard Version*

# The Bhagavad Gita
## Be Aware of Me Always

SRI KRISHNA:

He who is free from selfish attachments,
Who has mastered his senses and passions,
Acts not, but is acted through by the Lord.
Listen to me now, O son of Kunti,
How one who has become an instrument
In the hands of the Lord attains Brahman,
The supreme consummation of wisdom.

Unerring in his discrimination,
Sovereign of his senses and passions,
Free from the clamor of likes and dislikes,
He leads a simple, self-reliant life
Based on meditation, using his speech,
Body, and mind to serve the Lord of Love.

Free from self-will, aggressiveness, arrogance,
From the lust to possess people or things,
He is at peace with himself and others
And enters into the unitive state.

United with the Lord, ever joyful,
Beyond the reach of self-will and sorrow,
He serves Me in every living creature
And attains supreme devotion to Me.
By loving Me he shares in my glory
And enters into my boundless being.
All his acts are performed in my service,
And through my grace he wins eternal life.

Make every act an offering to Me;
Regard Me as your only protector.
Make every thought an offering to Me;
Meditate on Me always.

Drawing upon your deepest resources,
You shall overcome all difficulties
Through my grace. But if you will not heed Me
In your self-will, nothing will avail you.

If you say, "I will not fight this battle,"
Your own nature will drive you into it.
If you will not fight the battle of life,
Your own karma will drive you into it.

The Lord dwells in the hearts of all creatures,
And he whirls them round on the wheel of time.
Run to him for refuge with all your strength
And peace profound will be yours through his grace.

I give you these precious words of wisdom;
Reflect on them and then choose what is best.
These are the last words I shall speak to you,
Dear one, for your spiritual fulfillment.

Be aware of Me always, adore Me,
Make every act an offering to Me,
And you shall come to Me; this I promise.
Leave all other support, and look to Me
For protection. I shall purify you
From the sins of the past. Do not grieve.

Do not share this wisdom with anyone
Who lacks in devotion or self-control,
Lacks the desire to learn, or who scoffs at Me.

He who teaches this supreme mystery
Of the Gita to all those who love Me
Will come to Me without doubt. No one
Can render Me more devoted service;
No one on earth can be more dear to Me.

He who meditates on these holy words
Worships Me with wisdom and devotion.
Even he who listens to them with faith,
Free from doubts, will find a happier world.

Have you fully understood my message?
Are you free from your doubts and delusions?

ARJUNA:
You have dispelled my doubts and delusions
And made me ready to fight this battle.
My faith is firm now, and I will do your will.

Swami Omkar

# *Prayer for Peace*

Adorable presence,
Thou who art within and without,
    above and below and all around,
Thou who art interpenetrating
    every cell of my being,
Thou who art the eye of my eyes,
    the ear of my ears,
    the heart of my heart,
    the mind of my mind,
    the breath of my breath,
    the life of my life,
    the soul of my soul,
Bless us, dear God, to be aware of thy presence
    now and here.

May we all be aware of thy presence
    in the East and the West, in the North and the South.
May peace and good will abide among individuals,
    communities, and nations.
This is my earnest prayer.

*May peace be unto all!*

# Epilogue
## *The Message of the Scriptures*
by Eknath Easwaran

Every morning my spiritual teacher, my Grandmother, used to go to our ancestral temple to worship the Lord as Shiva. On her return she would place behind my ear a flower she had offered to the Lord in worship and bless me with these simple words: "May you be like Markandeya!"

Markandeya is an illumined teenager in the Hindu scriptures, whose parents prayed for a son who would be completely devoted to Lord Shiva. Their prayer was finally granted—but with the sad condition that their son would die on his sixteenth birthday.

The first word Markandeya lisped as a baby was "Shiva, Shiva." His love for the Lord grew from day to day until it filled his consciousness. When he attained his sixteenth birthday, he learned from his heartbroken parents that Yama, the King of Death, would be claiming him as his victim that day. On hearing this, Markandeya sat down in deep meditation at the feet of Lord Shiva, who is known in Sanskrit as *Mrityunjaya,* the Conqueror of Death.

At the appointed hour Yama appeared for his victim. But as he was about to carry him away, Lord Shiva arose in the depths of Markandeya's meditation to protect his young devotee. The Lord placed one hand on Markandeya's head in infinite love, and with the other he pointed his trident at the King of Death, who trembled like a leaf in the wind at the sight of Mrityunjaya.

"Don't you know," asked the Conqueror of Death, "that anyone who takes refuge at my feet has gone beyond your power? Markandeya has now become immortal through my grace."

It took years for me to understand that Markandeya's story is not poetry, fantasy, or philosophy. It is possible for every human being to go beyond the reach of death, not in some afterlife but here and now. And not only is it possible, it is our birthright.

This realization lies at the heart of mysticism everywhere. The instruction in the Bhagavad Gita and the Upanishads is clear, complete, and practical. You are neither body nor mind, both of which are subject to change. The body is your external instrument; the mind is your internal instrument. But you are the operator, the *Ātman* or Self. This Self is immutable, immortal, indivisible, infinite, the same in every creature. To realize the Self is to attain the supreme goal of life.

This is the purpose of meditation. Self-realization is beyond the senses and the intellect. It comes through a higher mode of knowing, developed through the sincere, systematic, sustained practice of meditation over many years. When the senses are stilled, when the mind is stilled, you are enabled through the infinite love of the Lord to become united with him in the supreme state of *samādhi*. To attain samādhi is to pass beyond death, to realize that you are immortal.

This deathless state of Self-realization can be attained by you while you are living right here on the face of this earth. As the medieval mystic Kabir puts it:

O friend, know Him and be one with Him whilst you live.
If you know Him not in life, how can you in death?
Don't dream that your soul will be united with Him
Because the body-house is demolished by death.
If He is realized now, He is realized then too;
If not, you go but to live in the Land of Death.

Lord Shiva is represented traditionally as the Divine Beggar, who comes with his begging bowl to your door for alms. When you offer this Beggar food, clothes, money, he refuses to accept them.

"What do you want from me then?" you ask.

"Your ego," comes the answer: "your selfishness, your separateness. Throw that in my bowl and become united with Mrityunjaya, Conqueror of Death."

The scriptures describe Lord Shiva as seated in *sahasrāra,* the thousand-petalled lotus, which may well be a spiritual symbol for the millions of cells that make up the human brain. In deep meditation there are many remarkable experiences that make you aware of this thousand-petalled lotus blooming in all its glory. In the stupendous climax of *samādhi,* you are enabled to wake up from the dream of being just a separate petal into the realization that you are the whole lotus, with the Lord of Love enshrined within it.

This is the message of every major scripture. It is the testimony of mystics everywhere, East or West. So I would like to offer this little anthology with the same blessing I received from my Grandmother, which still reverberates through my life: *Meditate. Realize the Self. Transcend death here and now. Become like Markandeya!*

# Notes on the Passages

21    *Prayer of Saint Francis*

Francis Bernardone, perhaps the best-loved of Christian saints, was born in Assisi, Italy, in 1181 or 1182. At the age of twenty-two, after a sudden illness that brought him almost to the point of death, he left his home and inheritance to follow an injunction that he felt he received from Christ himself: "Francis, go and rebuild my Church." Three great Franciscan orders quickly grew around the men, women, and lay disciples who responded to his joyful example of universal love and selfless service.

22    *Invocations to the Upanishads*

The Upanishads are probably the oldest mystical documents in the world. In written form they date from the second century before Christ; how long they were preserved before that in India's long oral tradition can only be conjectured. The invocations in this collection are associated with various Upanishads, often with more than one. Selections 1 and 2 have been translated by Eknath Easwaran; the others are from *The Upanishads: Breath of the Eternal,* translated by Swami Prabhavananda and Frederick Manchester (Hollywood: Vedanta Press, 1968).

24    *The Illumined Man*

These are the closing verses of the second chapter of the Bhagavad Gita ("Song of the Lord"), probably India's best-known scripture, a masterpiece of world poetry on which countless mystics have drawn for daily, practical guidance. The Gita is a dialogue between Sri Krishna, an incarnation of the Lord, and his friend and disciple Arjuna, a warrior prince who represents anyone trying to live a spiritual life in the midst of worldly activity and conflict. This translation is by Eknath Easwaran, from his *Bhagavad Gita for Daily Living* (Petaluma, California: Nilgiri Press, 1975– ).

26    *The Shema*

These three segments of the Torah have been recited together since Biblical times as the central affirmation of the Jewish faith. Tradition prescribes that the Shema be spoken "with entire collection and concentration of heart and mind." The translation is by Ellen Lehmann.

27    *Adon Olam* ["Lord of the universe"]

After the Psalms, this is perhaps the most popular hymn in the Jewish liturgy. Authorship is sometimes ascribed to the poet and mystic Solomon ibn Gabirol, who lived in Spain in the eleventh century. The translation is by Ellen Lehmann.

28    *Tao Te Ching*

A collection of verses about Tao—'the Way,' the indivisible unity—traditionally ascribed to the Chinese mystic Lao Tzu, who lived perhaps in the sixth century B. C. The translation is by Stephen Ruppenthal.

29    *Prayers from the Rig Veda*

The four Vedas are the oldest of the Hindu scriptures, with the Rig Veda the most ancient of all. Hymns, from which these two selections have been chosen, make up the first part of each Veda; in the latter parts are found the Upanishads. "God makes the rivers to flow" has been translated by Eknath Easwaran; "May we be united in heart," translated by Swami Prabhavananda and Christopher Isherwood, is from *Prayers and Meditations Compiled from the Scriptures of India,* cited above.

30 *Poems of Saint Teresa of Avila*

Teresa de Cepeda y Ahumada, born in Avila, Spain, in 1515, is one of the best-loved saints in the Catholic tradition and a spiritual figure of universal appeal. A vivacious, talented girl, she entered a Carmelite convent at eighteen and passed more than twenty years there in doubt and division before she was able to dedicate herself completely to God. After that her life is one of intense practical activity—establishing convents, teaching, writing, traveling—centered in the deepest spirituality and inner peace. These little poems were written without thought of publication. The most famous, "Let nothing disturb thee," was found in her breviary after her death. The translation is by James Wehlage.

31 *Hymn to the Divine Mother*

In the Hindu tradition the Lord is often regarded as possessing two aspects, one masculine, the other feminine. The latter, the creative power of the Godhead, is worshipped under several names as the Divine Mother of the universe. The hymn in this book is taken from the Chandi, a sacred book which sings the praise of the Divine Mother. The translation is by Swami Prabhavananda and Christopher Isherwood, from their *Prayers and Meditations Compiled from the Scriptures of India* (Hollywood: Vedanta Press, 1967).

32 *Twin Verses*

This is the opening chapter of the Dhammapada, a book-length collection of sayings in verse form which more than any other scripture bears the stamp of the Buddha himself. *Buddha*—literally 'he who is awake'—is the loving title given to the young prince Siddhartha Gautama (563–483 B. C.) after he attained *nirvāna* or Self-realization. For perhaps forty-five years the Buddha walked from village to village all over India, revitalizing ancient spiritual values. The translation is by Eknath Easwaran.

34 *The Wonderful Effects of Divine Love*

Selected from Book III, Chapter 5, of *The Imitation of Christ,* a book that has probably been read by and inspired more Christians than any other spiritual work except the Bible. Its traditional author, Thomas a Kempis (ca. 1380–1471), spent most of his life in Holland among the Brethren of the Common Life, a community devoted to a life of simplicity, selfless service, and the "imitation of Christ," in tumultuous times that fostered other notable European mystics: Saint Catherine of Siena, Henry Suso, Nicholas of Cusa. This translation, based on that of Anthony Hoskins (ca. 1613), is from The World's Classics, vol. 49, *Of the Imitation of Christ: Four Books by Thomas a Kempis* (London: Oxford University Press, 1903).

36 *The Katha Upanishad*

Tells the story of Nachiketa, a daring teenager who goes to the King of Death himself to get the secret of life. The selections in this book (Part I, Cantos 2 and 3) begin after Yama, who personifies the force of death, has tested Nachiketa's earnestness and found him worthy of instruction. The translation is by Eknath Easwaran; a full version is included in his *Dialogue with Death: The Spiritual Psychology of the Katha Upanishad* (Petaluma: Nilgiri Press, 1981).

45 *Discourse on Good Will (Metta Sutta)*

From the Sutta Nipata, a collection of dialogues with the Buddha said to be among the oldest parts of the Pali Buddhist canon. This translation is by Stephen Ruppenthal.

46 *Psalms*

King James Version. Psalms 22 and 23 are psalms of David.

48 *The Practice of the Presence of God*
From a letter by "Brother Lawrence" (Nicholas Herman), who lived almost sixty years as an obscure lay brother among the Carmelites in seventeenth-century Paris. The little collection of letters and conversations pieced together after his death in 1691, less than a week after this letter was written, is an underground classic of Christian devotion.

49 *Entering into Joy*
Augustine was born in North Africa in 354 and lived into the last stages of collapse of the Roman Empire. His *Confessions,* one of the world's great pieces of autobiographical literature, tells the story of a brilliant, passionate young man who learned to channel all his passions toward God. This translation from Book 9, Chapter 10, is by Professor Michael N. Nagler.

50 *The Isha Upanishad*
(See also entry for page 22, above.) Mahatma Gandhi said of this Upanishad that it "contains the summit of human wisdom." This translation is by Eknath Easwaran, from *Three Upanishads: Isha, Mandukya, and Shvetashvatara* (Berkeley: Blue Mountain Center of Meditation [Nilgiri Press], 1973).

52 *Invocations*
Abdullah al-Ansari, often referred to as Ansari of Herat, was a Persian poet and mystic in the Sufi tradition of Islam, who died in 1088. The verses collected here have been translated by Sardar Sir Jogendra Singh in *The Persian Mystics: Invocations of al-Ansari al-Harawi* (London: J. Murray, 1939).

57 *Four Things That Bring Much Inward Peace*
From Book III, Chapter 23, of *The Imitation of Christ* (see entry for page 34 above).

58 *The Central Truth*
Swami Ramdas was born Vittal Rao in Kerala, South India, in 1884 and took to the spiritual life when in his thirties. His long search for Self-realization is vividly described in three of his books: *In Quest of God, In the Vision of God*—from which this passage was taken—and *World is God* (Bombay: Bharatiya Vidya Bhavan, 1969, 1963, and 1967).

59 *The Whole World Is Your Own*
These words are revered as the last message of Sri Sarada Devi (1853–1920), "Holy Mother," wife of Sri Ramakrishna (see below) and helpmate in his work.

59 *The Path*
Mohandas K. Gandhi—usually in India called Mahatma Gandhi; the title means "great soul"—was born in British India in 1869 and died in January, 1949, having led his country to freedom through a nonviolent struggle based on love and selfless service. This passage is from a collection of his writings entitled *My Religion* (Ahmedabad, India: Navajivan, 1955).

60 *Believing in Mind*
Seng Ts'an (third century B.C.) is said to have been the Third Patriarch of Ch'an Buddhism, which passed into Japan as Zen. This translation is by Stephen Ruppenthal.

62 *The Way of Love*
Chapter 12 of the Bhagavad Gita, translated by Eknath Easwaran (see entry for page 24 above).

64 *The Sermon on the Mount*
The Gospel According to St. Matthew, 5:3–16, 43–48; 6:9–13.

69 *Christ Be with Me*
From a hymn traditionally ascribed to Saint Patrick, fifth century A.D.

70    *The Brahmin*
This is the concluding chapter of the Dhammapada of the Compassionate Buddha (see entry for page 32 above). *Brahmin* here is used in its root sense: "one who is worthy of knowing God [Brahman]." The translation is by Eknath Easwaran.

74    *Whatever You Do*
The concluding verses of Chapter 9 of the Bhagavad Gita, translated by Eknath Easwaran (see entry for page 24 above).

75    *The Kena Upanishad*
(See also entry for page 22 above.) *Kena* in Sanskrit means "by whom," the first word of the question with which it opens. This translation is by Eknath Easwaran.

76    *Poems of Kabir*
Kabir, a fifteenth-century Indian mystic, is one of the world's great poets. He is often claimed to be Hindu by the Hindus and Muslim by the Muslims because of the way his songs infuse the mysticism of the Upanishads with the Sufis' ecstatic love, but it would be truer to say he was too universal to be confined to one tradition. These translations are by another great Indian poet, Rabindranath Tagore, in *One Hundred Poems of Kabir* (London: Macmillan and Co. Ltd., 1967).

78    *Lord That Giveth Strength*
From *The Imitation of Christ,* Book III, Chapter 30 (see note for page 34 above).

80    *Songs of Sri Ramakrishna*
Sri Ramakrishna, one of the great figures in world mysticism, was born in Bengal, North India, in 1836. He taught, and lived out in his own life, that God can be realized within all the world's major religions if one seeks with completely unified desire. He worshipped God as the Divine Mother (see note for page 31 above). These songs, by different composers, are among the many that Sri Ramakrishna used to enjoy. They are selected from *The Gospel of Sri Ramakrishna,* by "M.", a disciple (New York: Ramakrishna-Vivekananda Center, 1942).

82    *The Shvetashvatara Upanishad*
Not numbered among the so-called principal Upanishads (see entry for page 22 above), the Shvetashvatara must be considered one of the most beautiful. It is dedicated to Shiva, the "Lord of Life," who represents God as the bestower of immortality. This selection includes part of Canto 1 and all of Canto 2. The translation is by Eknath Easwaran (*Three Upanishads,* cited above).

86    *Epistle on Love*
In his early days Saint Paul was Saul, a Jewish tentmaker in Tarsus soon after the time of Jesus, who persecuted the early Christians until he experienced a cataclysmic vision while traveling to Damascus. Afterwards he explained, "I am crucified with Christ: nevertheless I live; yet not I, but Christ liveth in me." He traveled and taught throughout Asia Minor and in Greece until his death in Rome, around 65 A.D.

88    *Be Aware of Me Always*
For practical purposes, these are the concluding verses of the Bhagavad Gita (18:49–73). The translation is by Eknath Easwaran, from *The Bhagavad Gita for Daily Living.*

89    *Prayer for Peace*
Composed by Swami Omkar, the venerable head of Shanti Ashram in Andhra Pradesh and of the Peace Center on the Nilgiris, South India.